Spare Change News Poems:

An Anthology by Homeless People and those Touched by Homelessness

editors:

Lee Varon
&
Marc Goldfinger

IBBETSON STREET PRESS
25 School Street
Somerville MA 02143

www.ibbetsonpress.com

ISBN 978-1-387-69009-1

Cover photo by Julia McElroy
Book design by S.R. Glines
text: Times New Roman

Each poet in this volume has a story to tell. Each voice is unique. Some of the poets here are homeless themselves, others work or volunteer with homeless people. Some of the poets here are moved by the plight of homelessness in our country.

The Guardian (2-2017) states that there are 549,925 homeless people in America. The homeless population is particularly severe in cities such as Boston with soaring real estate markets. Although people in shelters were included in this statistic, people in other situations—living in their cars, couch surfing, those who escape detection—were not counted.

The *Spare Change News* newspaper was founded in 1992 by a group of homeless individuals and a housed advocate. Since its inception, *Spare Change News* has worked to elevate the voices of homeless and economically disadvantaged people in the Boston area.

In these pages you will find the poetry of many people who are or have been homeless or have been touched in some way by homelessness. You will find the poetry of veterans, of those with mental health issues, of those struggling with substance use disorder. You will find poems written by incarcerated or formerly incarcerated people.

You will find poems of hardships here. There are poems about the hardships of living with poverty, racism, sexism, and homophobia and the hardships of dealing with abuse and neglect. But there are also poems of triumph, resilience and celebration.

Any profits from the sale of this volume will be donated to the Homeless Empowerment Project, which publishes *Spare Change News*.

We hope you will be touched and inspired by these poems.

— Lee Varon and Marc Goldfinger, Editors

*Note: When we began to work on this anthology we attempted to reach each poet and obtain biographical notes from them. Unfortunately, we weren't able to reach many people, therefore we chose not to include any bios.

Contents

Spare Change News Poems

Khalifa
Ayat al-Ghormezi

Hear me:
You, the elder,
the "good man," who "safeguards justice"
(so you have always declared),

if I were to make excuses for you,
I, for you,
for the things you have done,
I would only look the fool,
for you would continue in your ways,
and murder us as "traitors."

Hear me:
Hear us all, for we all demand likewise—
both sects, all Bahrainis:

You must go.
Take His Majesty with you,
and leave your deeds behind.

You, oppressor,
from where do you derive your power,
the power to keep your people down?—
all your people,
even women
even children
even men.
Yet you call for "dialogue,"
even in the midst of your brutality?

No! … No! …
One word: No!
One demand:
Give us back our Bahrain.
Return this country to its people;
to us, its people

Our Bahrain is ours.

The Fire King
Susan J. Allspaw

The pipes in the subway station fascinate him,
his boy-hands patting the cool skins
that run into the earth above him,
and he wonders how they stop fire.
He absorbs the closed spigots,
struggles to understand the power behind
the brightly painted valves
as the tingle of heat rises in his fingertips,
and he wants to feel it quenched.

He works it through:
like Prometheus he will learn
what it is like to feel the heat of burning;
he has watched the flickers dance, has
fallen in love with their motion,
the breathing of flames.
The blonde-haired boy wears his plastic fireman's cap
with pride, and does not understand
how the heat will hit him.
He does not know that when he grows alone,
it will creep out of his remains after the smoke has cleared,
the chill of his suspension on the Mount inching into him,
with scavengers pecking at his heart daily.

The little fire king has not yet moved
past the reach of his mother's hand
and will not feel the lick of flames suck his breath away.

Autumnal
Rusty Barnes

Green and gold, the way the light plays off the leaves.
Early autumn, hot—we've come from church.
We are in the water at the base of the Little Falls,
the cabin door open, your battery-operated boombox
blasting out Van Morrison, a water snake swims
panicked from our midst, you jump into my lap,
bang your arm against the rock and swear; the bruise
blooms quickly; I kiss your skin dry.

Later we climb the slick rocks of the Little Falls,
leave the fire behind in the dead-star night,
climb to the rocks of the Big Falls a mile up
the creek—your father will be expecting your
foot-sound soon—He drinks Schlitz by the door,
watches Carson after he's finished washing clothes.
If we could see through the trees and the hill we could
Watch him pop another can and wish for a wife.

Fading sound of an engine.
Slither of your jeans zipper.
Mossy smell of your hair in the crook of my elbow.
No sky is endless but the one before us.
We know there's no heaven, but wish anyway as we look up.
You hold your breath at every twig-crack.
We are naked on the rocks in the woods in Mosherville, PA
Waiting for God to show before your father does.

Stop Singing
Douglas Bishop

You cannot be singing for me man
are you thinking there is some jive in that tune
where the street is jumping up to meet you
smack in the face man
didn't you see the way her blood ran down into the gutter
and mixed with the gasoline
this is the new way to move man
what do you think you believe
when there's nothing to wait for
look in the trash cans
look at the gulls hanging around the dumpster in back of Church Street
look at the loading dock where the diesel is idling
there's no singing there man
no restitution to pay for the day
that still has me out in front of the seven eleven
panning for quarters
man you think you know where I live
but you have no idea
under the overpass
in between the edges of the city
in between the lines
of your mortgage payment and your credit card number
the days are not measured the way you're going man
you have to turn it inside out
go upside down
because there's another bite
another need
that doesn't have anything to do with that singing
you have no clue
what the dawn brings after being on the pavement all night
survival doesn't have a rosy-pink color
this is the edge of the street man

and it's ready to cut you out
because you have no idea what's coming down right now
so stop that stupid singing
and get to work

at the fish market
Zachary Bos

The octopuses in their plastic tub
darken the cold seawater they stew in
with expectorations of ink. They rub
against each other like lazy noodles.
One, lucky, topmost in the uncooked soup,
sees the purple urchins packed tight with ice
and writhes more urgently as if it could taste
in its imagination the sweet
red roe spilling from the split-open shell.
That's the one I point out to the monger:
Give me the dreamer. Let him be dreaming
of stalking the sweet roe over the coral
when I drop him boneless into the pot
so the salt of dreaming flavors the meal.

2 Suits
Martha Boss

my father had 2 suits.
he rotated them
all through
the 30's depression
and World War II.

when i was old enough to know how
my mother assigned me
to the job
of taking the suits
to the dry cleaner.

she would say
"now remember to say "pressed only".
or she would say
"tell them clean & press"
depending on how long he had worn it.

& i would memorize the instructions
all the way
saying the words over & over.

i hardly ever saw my father.
he worked at work.
then he drank in the tavern.
i got to know him through the suits.

he died
& they cremated him in one of them.
i'd like the other one to find him
& they both walk through my door.

2 suits,
pressed.
the ghost of my father.

Why I Ride
K. Peddlar Bridges

Why do I ride?

It's because of all those times
that I've stood at the curb
red-eyed—broken-hearted
lost soul'ed
and when that Harley engine fires
I can't remember—why?

Why do I ride?
It's because when I feel
that Harley tranny
slip into first ...

Lost money
wrecked cars
lost jobs
wrecked marriages
lost weekends
wrecked lives
all take second place
to the rush of first gear...

Why do I ride?
It's because the rumble
of Harley exhaust
has the echo of old rock bands
the beat of tribal drums
and the thunder
of horse's hooves
just a little ahead
of the angry posse

Why do I ride?
It's because at 60 mph
nobody can look over my shoulder
and ask—what's that?

Why do I ride?
It's because 80 mph
nobody can ask…

Who are you?
Where are you?
Where have you been?

NO! All they can do—is
twist their shoulders
snap their neck and ask…

WHAT WAS THAT?

Waiting for God
Jeff Brunner

The white demons have been playing
havoc with my angels all year.
Simon Weil, the French philosopher and mystic
called it, "the long winter's night sleep".

I call it acute depression—
my prozac gone wrong,
wanting to jump in front of a speeding bus.

Still, I wait on this rotting park bench
for relief, for a lifting of the spirit,
possibly even some grace, some light
as I watch snowflake after immaculate snowflake fall
from a pregnant December sky.

Miles Passed By
Bob "Bikerwolf" Bryant

Roads traveled, Lessons learned
Righteous Runs, Crash and Burns
Scarred body, Wounded Soul
Miles passed by as two wheels rolled

Friends enter, Friends leave
Sometimes happy, Sometimes peeved
Yesterdays passed, Feeling old
Miles passed by as two wheels rolled

Hopefully destined, To always roam
Ride with Brothers, Ride Alone
Always proud, Sometimes too bold
Miles passed by as two wheels rolled

Partied Hard, Worked hard too
Did my time, Paid my dues
Always broke, Never struck gold
Miles passed by as two wheels rolled

Winds blow, Feeling the breeze
Arms stretched, bended knees
Scarred body, Wounded soul
Miles passed by as two wheels rolled

Buzzard Affiliate

S.E. Casey

News chopper hovers
Rotor wash a dark heartbeat
Vultures circle prey

Lens a greedy eye
Colors world in a yellow
Journalistic glaze

Camera's rotten cuisine
Its powerful stomach acid
Digests all tragedies

Twenty four hour feeding
A carrion economy
Value created by scarcity
Famine becomes the feast

Faux cunning magic
A modern alchemy
Where the headline teaser
And the buried lead
Are converted into gold

Spare Change
Mia Champion

"I love your dress,
I love your hair,
I love everything about you."
clink-clanked from a shaky mouth
and his cup stood still.
I spared a glance and tossed my best smile
to a man who forgot to beg
from a woman who forgot
she had change.

Deer Stands
K. Chapman

A wild turkey
that buzzed across the road,
as we flew over hills
with red dirt spiraling behind,
made its way quick as a sweet dream,
while we drove through the hunting camp.

At Pelahatchie Bay
K. Chapman

From the banks of Turtle Creek
At the end of March
You can fish for
Big white perch
While the dogwoods drop
Big white blooms
All around you

In The Kingdom Of Nothing Much
Mary P. Chatfield

As in other countries
in the Kingdom of Nothing Much
there is a great divide.

Last week a tarp
was hidden among the bushes in the park
this week it has become a tent
compact a dark green
no one will notice until the leaves drop
a fallen branch planted nearby
like a flagpole
flying an invisible banner of defiance.

On a bench a ways off
someone is lying
head and torso
covered by an old army blanket
only the worn boots tell you
it's a body not a bundle.

Tentman works the traffic light on the parkway
homeless veteran his sign says
hard to resist
Benchman is a veteran too
but he gets the horrors at night
and is strengthless in the day
Tentman will have a bicycle one of these days
and ditch his shopping cart
Benchman won't last the year
someone will find him
frozen under a bridge
his identity his only possession.

Drunk Radio Poems
Dave Church

My radio has only two stations —
One classical, the other jazz.
When I drink,
I listen to classical.
When I write,
I listen to jazz.
Lately,
I've been drinking more
And writing less. So,
The other night,
I borrowed the landlady's radio.
I wanted to listen to both stations
At the same time.
I figured maybe then
I could drink
AND
Make a few poems.
When I woke up next morning,
I read them over and over and over.
None of them made any sense.
I typed them up anyway—
Submitted them to the New Yorker.

bagel bards
Joseph A. Cohen

The whiff of toasted bagels filled the air, yet not a poem was read.
Poets of every breed sat to breakfast while
easy talk danced to the drumbeat of seasoned writers.
Tales of praise or rejections were revealed.
Some wrote prose, others worked at poetry of the day.
Still there are those that edit or publish.
Minus an agenda, talk was open yet touched with humor.
What was the week like? Who said what? When do we eat?
Newly published books were passed around above
warm cheese Danishes and steaming hot coffee.
Groups huddled in circles, the more vocal holding forth.
The tradition so solid, the buzzing sounded in meter.
Rare is a scene so calm where the literary mingle without envy.
This, the Saturday morning for poets, is to be treasured.
Long live the songs of Bagel Bards artists.

(Untitled)
Janet Cormier

She wrote and wrote and wrote
And for all her efforts collected piles of rejection letters
Some kind
Some generic
Some very bitter and acidic
But she wrote and she wrote and she wrote
Notebooks full of poems and stories about people, things, ideas
Then one day it seemed that the words stopped
She tried to find them
She prayed for their return, even went into therapy to find them
Only to realize the therapists were more intrigued by her story than her dilemma!
The words taunted her, whirled around her
But none could be captured or coaxed to linger or sit on a page

Maybe it was all the disappointments…
The details of everyday life being too much
Years passed but there were no words written on paper,
Unless you count her signature on checks and lists of things to do
Sometimes she tried to call to them
But the words were stubborn and would not return
It seemed that the decades led into centuries
One day the words returned
Casually, barely noticed
Appearing first on crumbled pages and then filling notebooks
Now they are reunited, she and her words
And she writes and she writes and she writes

RUN & TELL IT:
LETTER TO LITTLE GIRLS (&BOYS)
Gayle Danley
from <u>NAKED</u>

If

the hug lasts too long
and you feel squeezed in
places private
places only you should see
Run and Tell It

If
the look turns into a stare
that makes you feel like
running and hiding
like disappearing
Run and Tell It

If
the room grows hot
and tight
and someone comes toward you wrong
(uncomfortably)
when you two are alone
Run and Tell It

If
you are touched
pinched
rubbed
brushed
felt
hit
spanked
and your heart screams
NOOOO: THIS IS NOT RIGHT
Run and Tell It

**Run Run Run
and Tell It**

even if you're told not to
even if you're not sure what has happened
even if it's someone you love
even if you're afraid
even if you're just a baby, a teenager, a woman

Run and Tell It
and in the likely event you're called a liar

Run and Tell It…
anyway

the telling makes you free

What I'm Made Of
Kathy Engel

I am a crab I am
chemical dispersant
spill, I am spilled
spilling, fish swelter
stone, I am slick, eyes
burn bleed oil, nose
oiled mucous, talk
spits from my oil
swollen lips, gurgle
and sputter drip from
my ears, crude ruts
my cheeks, neck scar
leaks oil, hair sheens
nipples weep yellow
colostrum oil, my
gut gasses, hips sling
through oil, thighs, wrists
calves oiled, ovaries
discharge oil, ankles
shellac shells, feet
smudge oil, I cough
up oil, skate oil loose
oil bowels, dna splits oil
blood scabs oil
bay of oil fin of oil rooster
crowing oil crow cawing oil
oh crab, oh oil of bird

HOW WE COULD HAVE LIVED OR DIED THIS WAY
Martin Espada

Not songs of loyalty alone are these,
But songs of insurrection also,
For I am the sworn poet of every dauntless rebel the world
over.
  — Walt Whitman

I see the dark-skinned bodies falling in the street as their ancestors fell
before the whip and steel, the last blood pooling, the last breath spitting.
I see the immigrant street vendor flashing his wallet to the cops,
shot so many times there are bullet holes in the soles of his feet.
I see the deaf woodcarver and his pocketknife, crossing the street
in front of a cop who yells, then fires. I see the drug raid, the wrong
door kicked in, the minister's heart seizing up. I see the man hawking
a fistful of cigarettes, the cop's chokehold that makes his wheezing
lungs stop wheezing forever. I am in the crowd, at the window,
kneeling beside the body left on the asphalt for hours, covered in a sheet.

I see the suicides: the conga player handcuffed for drumming on the subway,
hanged in the jail cell with his hands cuffed behind him; the suspect leaking
blood from his chest in the back seat of the squad car; the 300–pound boy
said to stampede barehanded into the bullets drilling his forehead.

I see the coroner nodding, the words he types in his report burrowing
into the skin like more bullets. I see the government investigations stacking,
words buzzing on the page, then suffocated as bees suffocate in a jar. I see
the next Black man, fleeing as the fugitive slave once fled the slave-catcher,
shot in the back for a broken tail light. I see the cop handcuff the corpse.

I see the rebels marching, hands upraised before the riot squads,
faces in bandannas against the tear gas, and I walk beside them unseen.
I see the poets, who will write the songs of insurrection generations unborn
will read or hear a century from now, words that make them wonder
how we could have lived or died this way, how the descendants of slaves
still fled and the descendants of slave-catchers still shot them, how we awoke
every morning without the blood of the dead sweating from every pore.

Barge
Kirk Etherton

A woman is the tugboat,
legs churning at the stern
of the shopping cart that's
burdened with plastic bags swelling
ripe to bursting with
returnable containers now
returning. Push comes to

push again, short-haul transport
(after looking long) of currency-in-waiting;
trickle-down-and-over economics.
Four small black rubber wheels
of commerce are turning,

turning through growing
pavement puddles, over glistening
sewer grates, propelled by this
one-humanpower engine straining
steadily upstream against
the rushing, splashing cars.

Sheer Ego!
Brian C. Felder

it's all meaningless
in the larger scheme of things
in the long view of history
but
since we don't have that angle on ourselves
what we do
what we say
what we think
is all the meaning we have to give to our lives

it's no wonder that we build monuments to
ourselves
statues
that the passing years render silly
and pigeons call home

Games
Ed Galing

in our old age,
my wife and i
played these
strange games,
it didn't begin
until we were in
our late eighties,
when my wife began
to say,
i am an old lady now,
and you are an old man,
i would smile and say,
i can spell good,
i can spell right
in two ways,
and she would begin to
spell WRITE...
and then RIGHT...
i would applaud and
say, that was very well done...
she would smile back and
say, see, i told you i
could spell...
never doubted it for
a minute, i would say,
now here is one for you
   how much is
ONE plus ONE?
   she would wrinkle
her brow as if in thought,
then suddenly chuckle and
say, ELEVEN....

it never failed to make
me laugh, too…i never
even thought of alzheimers…
    aahh, the games that
we once played in our old age.

Harmonica
Ed Galing

i learned to
play the
"hohner harmonica"
when i was a young boy

now i am ninety
alone since my
wife died

in the summer i
sit in the
nearby park
and play the harmonica

it makes me feel so good
to play songs long out of
fashion

world war two music
when war seemed like
a holy mission

young and old
pass me by
as i sit there
white hair
bent over

and the songs
come out and it's
me at twenty

my wife kissing me
before i left
for the army to
fight for democracy
a word now gone.

UNTITLED
Steven J. Gallo

So what of love today
When terror stalks the
Human souls
As men and women
Fear for the religion
Of death upon their
Doorsteps.
(Out of night's blackness
The dawn still comes
Bringing light into
This world.)
It is fear that
Thunders through

Barren forests and
Leaf strewn fields.
Alone, isolated
Within the cuticle of
Self there are no
Defenses, no amulets
To bring to bear,
No pentacles to hide
Within.
i watch, i wait
For the truth of
Compassion to finally
Fill the souls of

This world, break
Bindings of isolated
Beings trembling
Beneath the
Weight of religion's
Fear.
i watch, i wait.
It is not that fears
Will disappear
But that the
Breath of life will
Restore to the world
The beauty of being.

Under the Poetry Line
From a misread headline: "Under the Poverty Line"
Harris Gardner

"Mister, can you spare a poem?"
A ragged soul mouths a snaggle-toothed plea.
"I haven't written a good line in a month."
You can relate to that with your angst
If you allow just one week to lapse.

You dig deep and offer a haiku.
"Sorry, but it's all I can give right now.
I hope it will help you make do."
His eyes peer from a grizzled face.
He moans in despair, "I'm famished.
A haiku won't fill a sandwich."

You pause for a beat. "It's better than a couplet."
His stomach rumbles, grumbles and groans.
"A savory sonnet would nicely sweeten my palate."
A fragile rasp rattles his voice.
Spectral fingers grasp his throat.
He doesn't take note; his words malinger.

At a nearby java shop, you buy him a hot cup
Of verse. It doesn't satisfy his thirst.
"Mister," his rhythm now ghastly thin,
"Can you spare some ink? My pen is dry."

Louisiana Letter
Andrea S. Gereighty

This poem; it's endless
like shopping in Schwegman's,
Prof queries Where's your resolution?
I haunt the mail carrier
where's your letter?

My daughter called Sunday from college
said snakes swim in a river like dogs
lacking only paws
I gave Goodwill my encyclopedia
picture pages glossy with snakes
I wanted to touch when I was little.
Deni saw a diamondback cross the Huzzah
in half an hour.

I talked two hours in West Virginia
about naming rivers
couldn't discover where
Monongahela came from
or why I haunt the mailman.

Some days I applaud my self for
not thinking of you till evening.
I don't think of poems.
At dawn, I rush from dreams
glazed with the crust of sleep
fall headlong into the closet
thrash about for the scrapbook
that picture of Eldoreque in the studio
before a thirty-eight in her mouth
discharged, bloodied Camp Gris-Gris
drove Jerry to guilt; to saying
the camp is haunted.

Write me: I'm frantic
I look in vain for:
The rhythm, the scrapbook, the contrasts
your letter.
the pressure; it's building
like this poem.

to june in lieu of flowers
Bruce Goldberg

In that little house far from the road
you made new left casserole and waited
while we marched on the induction center
and drove all night across the western slope
to Grand Junction the day
King was killed.

I still see you in your long blue denim dress,
a frontier wife of the sixties and later, after monogamy
lay smashed into the separate pieces
of our lives and you and John split,
you still smiled and the casserole was
as good as ever.

I knew you were going to die, we all did,
but we kept it far away in a quiet distance,
because you wanted it there.

Finally, we lost touch and never found it again
except asleep in the collective fist of memory
where it remains the only touch we ever keep —
the smell of a casserole, the small house,
the blue denim of the dress,
the last smile of goodbye.

A Couple Of Kids
Marc D. Goldfinger

She sits in front
of the 7-11, a cup
for spare change in
her hand. Her eyes are

still clear. He comes out
of the store, I've seen them
together before. She is quite
young, maybe 17 years old, he is

quite high on heroin, possibly early
20's, heavy lidded eyes, he scratches
his nose. "We're going to get married,"
he says to me as he hands her a cardboard

sign to hold that says, "broke and hungry,
please help." "I just don't have the cash for
the ring yet," is what he says as he looks at me
with pinned eyes. She says, "Maybe we'll go to

Florida where the nights are warm. When we get
the money." He sits
next to her, closes his
eyes, his head tips forward.

She places her arm around his
shoulders. "I got me a good one,
eh," she says with a big smile, wide
innocent eyes. I don't know what to

say. I want to shake her, wake her up
from whatever keeps her asleep. Her eyes

are still clear, he hasn't turned her on to the
heroin yet. I can still see them, sitting
in front of the 7-11 in the heart
of Central Square. They

haven't got to Florida yet.

They're still sitting there.

Eternity
Joe Gouveia

A seagull died today
Where I was working
To support my art
On someone else's boat
In Hyannis Harbor

The seagull was sitting
On a piling
I was scrubbing twin hulls
You could say we both were
Catching suntans problem was
By mid-day that bird was beak-down

In the harbor
Later some kids came
Barreling down the docks
Canon-balled into the water
Flocked toward that gull
Poking it to see how it died

One kid wanted to throw
The carcass up onto the dock
So as to get a closer look at Death
Or maybe they were just
In a hurry to grow up

Or something like that or
Something like that

THE WAGE SLAVE
Carolyn Gregory

They never listened
as they raved about their trips
to Paris, paid for a Mercedes
to roam the countryside.

They never acknowledged
how messages were written
with perfect grammar
between Boston and Singapore,
offering a recommendation
for someone invisible.

They did not care
that she worked with bronchitis,
ignoring slammed doors,
ducking loud Russian and German

and she did what she was told to do,
putting her life on hold
again for someone else.

behind the wall
Emmanuel Guerrir

BROKE THE LAW NOW I'M BEHIND THE WALL
ALL OF A SUDDEN, I'M WRITING POEMS BEHIND THE WALL
EVEN WROTE A BOOK, BEHIND THE WALL
MAYBE CAUSE I THINK MORE, BEHIND THE WALL
I'M A DISTANT MEMORY, BEHIND THE WALL
LIFE CAN'T BE HARDER THEN, BEHIND THE WALL
BASKETBALL HOPES FADED IN THE BIG YARD, BEHIND THE WALL
I BECAME A MAN, BEHIND THE WALL
MY CHILDREN WERE BORN, WHILE I WAS BEHIND THE WALL
GROWN MAN WITH A CURFEW, BEHIND THE WALL
NO SOURCE OF INCOME, BEHIND THE WALL
INMATE #121136, BEHIND THE WALL
FINALLY READY TO LIVE BEYOND THESE WALLS

first and last taste
Emmanuel Guerrir

MY FIRST TASTE WAS AT AGE 8
I REMEMBER HOW SWEET YOU TASTED
RAMEN NOODLES, BUG JUICE & D-REPORTS THINGS I TRULY HATE
ALL MY 20'S YEARS I'VE WASTED
FELLOW ADDICTS, TRUST ME I CAN RELATE
WE ONLY WANTED FUN, BUT I GOT INCARCERATED
I'M 32 NOW, AND ALMOST GRAY
ANOTHER BIRTHDAY MY DRINKING TOOK AWAY
I BRAG BOUT MY 3.7 GPA
ALCOHOL LEVEL .242 SHATTERED THAT PLATE
PROBATION VIOLATION O.U.I. 2ND OFFENSE THAT'S MY CASE
18 MONTHS IN BILLY IS MY STAY
WHEN I THINK ABOUT ONE LAST TASTE
I REMEMBER BECAUSE OF YOU, CANTEEN IS EVERY THURSDAY

Westwood Lodge, 1980 –1990
Sarah Hannah (1967 – 2007, R.I.P.)

Apt. 1

And once again you go west, to that perennial
Resort at the end of the bending street, row of pines,
Where Sexton strolled through noon, made moccasins,
And danced in a circle: the Summer Hotel.

Why every tumid season, cicadas burning blue,
Beetles mounting one another, chewing all the flowers,
Do your pupils pinpoint, and your breath sours?
I call the police, who've nothing else to do.

"Safest city in America" (or so our town's ordained);
They arrive in flashing squadrons: at least eleven
Armed, sturdy men, five cars, for one uneven,
Overly-sedated woman past sixty. You've downed

Some sedatives with wine. How many? Your swoon
Gives none away; the Xanax bottle lies beneath the bed
With cigarettes and nylon stockings, so your stomach's pumped
Just in case. You always make it known to someone

Swiftly after it's been done: you will be saved. Inside,
Double-locked, you wait in line to use the phone. (Twenty-five
Years later, I still dream you're calling; you're alive,
Away someplace, but a vast conspiracy of bureaucrats hides

You from me. I wake, cry out. What does it mean, and where?)
Back then you reached me, asked for cigarettes,
Stockings, underwear, and the small two-volume set
Of Redon (ed. Rosaline Bacou). It doesn't matter

That the text's in French—it's got color plates.
While you're gone I have the house to myself,
Turn the radio up, sing to the bookshelves,
Across the stucco arches to the ceiling's walnut

Beams: Jay and the Americans' "This Magic Moment,"
With some irony but not quite as much
As one might think, considering the lawn's gone thatch,
Burned brown, you're in lock up, and my paycheck's spent.

Speaking of lawns, ours was once all sun and dapple.
Childhood. A man mowed, a woman watered.
Something had to rot, go sour; someone ate the apple.
God died in the yard, a la Soren Kierkegaard —

In the doom of the downward slash: Existentialism
One-Oh-One, for frosh, I lie out and rub
Baby oil on my legs, hope to burn. God's a white grub.
He ate the lawn, but we can't afford to exterminate him.

Upside: you can't yell at me for wasting time lying
In the sun (to please a man?). Downside: the docs
Tell me each time you come back in, they'll lock You up
for longer. If this crazy summer torquing

Doesn't stop, they'll put you somewhere else
For good (when we've run through the insurance) —
An institution of the state. No moondance,
Cakewalk. Or maybe dancing all the time in circles.

But for now, the asylum grass we walk on's trimmed,
Thick and green. We watch the sky from Adirondack
Chairs. I bring flowers—cosmos, phlox, and hollyhock,
Your favorite—from our garden. Then, on a whim

One day, I arrive early to your delight; I'm the only one,
After all, who comes. I've packed your acid-free
Paper and watercolors, though you didn't ask. Forgive me,
You say, I'll paint planets. Best thing I could have done.

Where is God?
Jim Haygood

God is on the streets,
God sleeps in the cold,
God eats whatever is found or given,
God drinks from a brown paper bag,
God smokes crack,
God has tracks,
And warms herself by barrels of fire,
God sleeps wrapped in tattered blankets,
On sidewalks and abandoned spaces,
God lives in the shadows,
And in the Light,
God fights for a place in line,
God hopes for a warm shower,
God is looking for work,
God has compassion,
God is sharing a sandwich,
God hopes for a break,
God prays for miracles,
God sees reality,
God sees right through us,
As we walk right by,
Looking for God.

THE BOTTOM LINE
Everett Hoagland

Lo, and behold!
Our would be bold
new president —

nominated, campaigned for,
elected by a mainstream
political
party,

by a mainstream political process
to head our (inter-) national
mess —

is neither a comrade, a mes-
siah,
nor magician.
Not even

the so-called American
Dream
in fruition. Heavens!
Unprecedented.

Imagine!
Of all things, President
Obama
is a politician.

HIROSHIMA
Everett Hoagland

lit candles glow through
tiny paper lantern boats
afloat on silence

Artstetten Und Mauthausen
Burton R. Hoffmann

Today we left the Donau Prinzessin
At the dock in Vienna,
For an outing by bus
To visit the castle in Artstetten
Owned by Franz Ferdinand.
More of interest to Austrians
Than Americans, I fear.
His assassination triggered
The start of World War I.
The end of the Hapsburg Era.

After lunch a visit to Mauthausen,
A Nazi concentration camp of World War II,
Where Jews, Gays and Unluckies
Were starved,
Brutally beaten,
Forced to labor at the quarry
Until they dropped.
Grim, austere buildings.
Remarkable modern sculptures though,
In commemoration.
The film we were shown
So moving,
All of us bathed in tears.

Doug Holder's Furnished Room
Newbury Street, Boston 1978-2003
Doug Holder

The raw, coiled
red glare
of the hot plate

the urine stain
of a sink
and the waft
of Red Sauce
from Davio's below

The head
a short anxious scamper
down the hall

the hacking cough
of the retired civil servant
through a thin wall.

And the spinster
who peers from
the crack in her door
gathers her pennies
and courage
for her big trip
to the corner store,

the wooden ladder that
ascended to a tar roof
the sweet/sorrow scent of city, rain and sea…
and my youth…

The Mugging: Times Square: 1973
Doug Holder

New Year's
I drank quarter beers
and lived in a delirium of lights.
The flash of the
flash-in-the pan
the hooker and the tourist
whores working the
opposite side of the street.

And then
running down
the dark alley
the sucker punch
the spray of American Express Checks
the denominations,
flapping to the ground
my face on the pavement
meeting a winding stream of
my own blood.

The war hoops
of the 125 Street
"Savage Skulls"

and my face
in the YMCA mirror
a purple distorted bruise
an impostor
a face
I would
never loose.

DEATH ROW
Alexis Ivy

Texas has taken the last meal away.
Inmates were asking too much.
The people they murdered
didn't ask for a last meal.
They, meaning the man who asked
for an olive, just one olive with the pit
still in it. The man who asked for a
pound of strawberries, candy bars,
Take 5's, Mary Jane's, a king-size
Milky Way. A plea for sugarless
pie with vanilla ice cream – melted,
every detail reported
in the Dallas Observer, how
they took their eggs, beaten
and scrambled, over-easy,
sunny-side-up and cage-free,
their steak prepared rare.
Indiana gives their condemned
a last meal three days
prior to execution because they are
expected to lose their appetite by
the final hours. The man who asked for
a vegetable pizza to be given to a home-
less person in Nashville. The felon
who wanted a plate of dirt.
Requests denied.

Lesbian Action Hero Rap
Mephistoles Johnson

She's a Jill on top of the hill-she doesn't need Jack
In fact
She's like the rabbit at the dog track,
My money's always on her, (no one can match her)
The dogs all chase her, but they never catch her.
no one can resist her - she don't need a mister
She's my sister
She's not somebody's daughter or somebody's wife
you talk that junk she might take your life
She's a poet, a lover, a dancer, a thespian
She's my sister and yeah, she's a lesbian.

Death of A Small Town
Chopper Kate

the wind recalls the ghostly sounds
of old train whistles in my hometown.
they ripped the steel rails from the ground,
all in the name of progress?
Severed, like a artery to a limb,
the town's life blood trickles crimson,
down the leaf clogged gutters.
Echoes of souls and feet
that passed, were witnessed
by buildings on the old main street.
Shuttered, boarded, blinded,
these icons of another time.
Speak to me in a voice of
rusted nails and old brick tumbling.
Musty and foul breath of a dying town,
cries out through the decay and crumbling,
"Remember Me!"

Where I Grew Up
Aminata Keita

Because I've always been quiet
Writing my poems
They always want to know
Where I grew up

I grew up in the projects
Where rich families
Don't allow their kids to visit

I grew up where you can't sleep at night
Because your neighbor and her boyfriend
Are busy making love and smoking marijuana

I grew up in a place
Where you'd wake at 10 am
On Sundays to the smell of omelets and coffee

Where I shared a room with my sisters
And we were known as the only family
Who spoke Mandigo

Where people take from those who don't have
And leave your pockets empty
Broke and more sad

I grew up where you can't tell the difference between
The kid who just graduated college and the local
drug dealer
They both look alike and can't get jobs, the odds

I grew up where the police would check you
Whenever they want
Without a warrant or probable cause

Where I grew up
Even the dead have to wait
Until their number is called

I grew up in a beautiful place
Often wondering as I looked up
At the moon shining over me
Questioning what it meant to me
Whether or not it was full

Where did I grow up?
That's where I grew up
What about you?

Citizen's Arrest
Alexander Levering Kern

Sometimes even now when I dip my toe
into the asphalt seas of Brattle Street
I recall my grade school fear of arrest.
Jaywalking is a serious crime,
our older brother Chris intoned
with whatever measure of wisdom comes
from six extra years on earth.

So we trembled, our anxious eyes darting both ways
before dashing across the gulf of Fessenden Street.
Citizen's arrest! Chris would cry, invoking the authority
of the DC police, and if that weren't enough,
the FBI. Looking out over the mansions of Cambridge now
I wonder who's watching my tentative step.
I laugh at the voice of my memory inside me,

shouting Hand's up, bud! It's a citizen's arrest!
remembering my new fear of cardiac arrest,
and before long I'm tallying the many small crimes
for which some people say there's no recompense:
a bad toupee daring to jog along the river,
an invisible man pitching his tent beside a park bench,
squirreling supplies for a summer on the streets,

the undocumented bodies across the road
erecting banquet tents for Harvard commencement
as billowing crimson robes stroll by.
Citizen's arrest! I cry out loud, launching my body
into the strange world of filial fear and ancient law
just waiting to be transgressed.

Shopping Cart: The Art of Steering
Alexander Levering Kern

At rush hour she fords the slick city street

dodging the metallic sharks.
Defiantly she guides her lifeboat to
the other side, weighed down by her cargo
of soda cans & peddler clothes.
Dressed today in her Sunday's best,
her life is hovering somewhere inside
her fraying overcoat.

Slowing my madcap rush to work

I press pause, to pay my respects.
Today she won't be moved, for nobody.
A moment later, though, the cart's alone
floating in midstream, damming it all,
and I wonder: is this life always best
pushed ahead, or sometimes,
is it best dragged behind?

nightshade
Linda Larson

A night on the streets is full of surprises that don't suit you and gifts you can't return. I find myself on my own at dusk in scenic, drug-ridden Central Square, in need of a bed, a meal and some Wild Irish Rose.

One ill-kept secret of the streets is the smell of shoes worn 24/7. Whether I am slipping onto a barstool at Sullivan's Tap on the arm of a white-haired old gentleman flashing a wad of twenties at me, or kneeling beside the communion rail, the putrid rot of my shoes is a shout-out to predators, 'This woman is homeless, helpless.'

Couch surfing is over-rated. It starts out fine. I have some money from stemming to share with friends who are getting high. It's going to be a deathly cold night outside the peephole.

In the wee hours there comes a chance for me to bring in some money. "Be nice to this guy," my pals tell me. "He likes you and look he's spending money. He'll get you high. He'll get all of us high."

It's not a choice for me to go back to where I was living unless I want yet another pair of black eyes. I tell everyone I'm fine, they're only shiners. I laugh it off. I'm a raccoon.

If I had it in me to kill him, I would.

It's 5:30 in the morning. I am out on the street feeling lucky to be outside in the fresh air. I would feel luckier if I had made it out with my jacket. There is enough change in my pocket for a large coffee regular…enough to buy me a seat in a warm place until the streets fill up and I can stem for more. It's so cold outside the passers-by on the street won't want to stop and fill the jangle in my cup. My bones ache.

Mom O Mom O Mom O Mom
Linda Larson

Measles weren't so bad. You running up and down
The stairs from the beauty shop, wooing me to get
Better with ice cold coca-cola on the rocks and a straw,
One sip at a time. White cotton gloves covered up the angry
Spots on my hands. We played twenty questions in the
Evening. The doctor has said no reading.
It was like a party and I was the guest du jour.

My green parakeet, Pete, flew out the screen door.
My sobbing hurt my throat. You went way out on a limb,
Promised me you would find him. Later, you returned
Carrying a little paper carton, the kind chop suey comes in.
You sat beside me on the couch and let me feel him fluttering inside.
I could almost feel his heart beating.
You told me he had been perched outside,
Clinging to the window of the pet store
Right downstairs, next to the beauty shop.
I believed you.

You could be quite a spectacle yourself
When you slipped into a gala outfit with a pin
On your lapel that scraped my cheek (just a bit),
A sparkle of red across your mouth, Revlon Fire and Ice,
You, posture perfect, three-inch heels taller,
Towering over my bed, fragrant with bourbon,
Cigarette smoke and Tabu. I couldn't
Let this apparition disappear, I howled
When you tried to loosen my arms,
You couldn't let me go either, began
To howl yourself. Dad disentangled us
Before your platinum meringue of a beehive
Came all to pieces.

Upon Hearing of Your Death in Your 34th Year

Linda Larson
  for Mike Amado

I fear losing your brightness to shades of memory,
the way you lean forward when you are being kind,
which is all the time,
the way you build your poetry in spades
and it comes out in hearts,
The way the drum beats our hearts beat the words beat.

Within the hour,
I dig into my box of childhood treasures, so insignificant now,
for two polished Winged Victories for your eyelids,
to pay Chiron's fee and then dredge up three
lint-covered Valiums for Cerberus,
who like a good dog will eat Anything.
I am worrying that if you can't translate
into three languages on a good day
you might end up excluded from
The Elysian Fields Anthology.

Nobody's fault you grew up grappling
with a pain shaking you by the balls
over a cliff, each breath reminding you
when the pain stopped you would be dead,
a promise it kept (like a heartless sundial ever
burnishing the Spoken Warrior's words.)

There is a question poetry asks of common sense:
Is it our language that leaves us incredulous
of any reality that doesn't measure itself
by a beginning and an end?
Is Plath's Ariel simply a nightlight
in a black, chaotic universe?
Ah, there's the rub.
Who was it exactly named the stars?
The constellations? and would that be enough?
To live on in that way? When art crosses the line
becoming myth you might oh so quickly
forget the name of this young poet.
But I would be happy to remember this line
of poetry on any battlefield life takes me,
in any last breath if there were time,
"There is a river I call Sky."

upstairs is the other side of the tracks
Linda Lerner

line I keep crossing without getting anywhere
like that stretch of tracks I stumbled on
crossing Fort Hamilton Parkway down streets
gentrifying toward a new grocery
sprung out of an old factory building

tracks that abruptly begin and end
like the response it came from upstairs
to justify a change of procedure
takes me nowhere…

a few trolleys rust along the tracks
near an outdoor café
a few feet from where I'd been,
closer to the river edged by a steep incline
of rocks and boulders reminded me of Maine
unleashing pirates and a captain from there
whose schooner they plundered a century ago
docked here in Red Hook*: the name
flings me to a water front bar
sailors flying on rum to mermaids
gangs roaming streets for treasure
landlords now seize

there were states lines I crossed
to be with a married man who crossed America
several times trying to leave home

a street I wasn't allowed
to cross as a child
but did anyway to visit a friend
on one of those tree lined big house blocks
I'd pretend was mine till I heard
doors slam angry words, a woman crying
and no longer believed
I'd ever crossed over to anything

*computer geeks invent a game called Red Hook's Revenge

Untitled
Daniel E. Levenson
from the book "Are These My Lions" written in Israel

Where is the nearest bomb shelter?
Good question.
I found one the other night,
in an apartment building
behind the café—
walk down the alley,
it's number three on the left,
go up the stairs, make a right,
it's on the left—
but sometimes it's locked

On Emek Refaim
life goes on as usual,
the shops and restaurants,
tourists and locals,
English and Hebrew,
the jazz festival

All these things
fill the cool summer evening,
no hint of fear

But still, you asked about the bomb shelter —
it is quiet down there,
I imagine,
silent,
waiting.

Renaissance
Bill Lord

A celebration of freedom
Released from bondage of addiction
Pill, bottle, needle, pipe
Clear-eyed and part of life
Again able to choose

Endless dirge, lost lovers
Booze and drugs now gone
Like dead best friends
No longer there to numb
Fear, doubt and insecurity.

The drinking problem ceased
Now become a thinking problem
Half full, half empty
Value the new freedom or
Dwell on lost oblivion.

Even a light switch
Moot if not flicked on
Curse and rant, darkness
Or stand, be part of
Today in the light.

Suffered long and alone
Life ruled by a fool
Got sober to feel better
Put aside past misery
Focus on the upside light.

Each new day dawns
Options for the sober mind
Part of the solution
Or part of the problem
I get busy living.

Father Bill's

Kathleen M.

Big boots, no matter the weather,
packs humped high on the back,
every morning between 7:30 and 8:00
they cross the Southern Artery.
Tortoises transporting the whole house:
underwear, socks, a flannel or two,
cigs, maybe a headphone.
Maybe some snuff, a couple of handkerchiefs,
a blue or red bandanna. A snapshot —
before the drugs took over, the teeth went bad,
before the person on the left left.
Wallet, flat as a dime.
Shuffling in two's and three's, early
mornings, they cross the causeway.
McDonald's beckons: hot coffee, if
the wait staffer's sympathetic.
Or the deep reeds of marsh grass behind the car wash;
the cemetery, with its do-nothing
roads, its ill-advised timepiece.
Used to be the library, quiet niche of the reading room,
deep brown sling-back chairs — read,
snooze. Patrons complained.
Hoping the sun will stay high, exercising its presence,
like shiftless gulls in the wind, they cross,
eyes averted.
Curbside: at the sign that points to the dog pound,
their homeless-home next door to the throwaways —
purebreds, mutts, the many cats — they wait.
When the pound incinerates the strays
that never make it to a family,
one detects an acrid smell.

At Aversboro Coffee Shop
Valerie Macon

an old man sits hunched over coffee
gazing into its blackness,
its curl of steam winding and vanishing.
His icy fingers, knotty as scrub oak,
embrace the cup. Nursing an apple
muffin, he pinches off morsels,
savoring the sweetness of musical chatter
from a nearby table where a giddy crowd of teens
huddle over smoothies and tomorrow's plans.

Apostrophe
Jennifer Martelli

Excuse me,
I'm trying to save my life.

I need to dodge the devil's stare —
he's been trying to catch my eye again.

And so, yes, I'm going to pray.

There is a star
I wish on every morning, Venus or

Lucifer the light giver. If I've wished once
on a star for you to come back, I've wished

a hundred times. If I've prayed once
in 20 sober years, I've prayed a thousand times.

And so, let's have a staring contest,

you and I, because we can't be honest.
I'll wrap this blanket around me and wish or pray.

I prayed to be rid of you.
I pray to be rid of you still.

There is no relief in any of this.

The Tale of Lost Innocence
Matthew Martinez

The risk of OD never crossed
Joey's mind; until my brother's
dead body
was discovered, as the
morning sun began to shine.

He called for me and
I came running. Joey knew
the risk of dying, and
he held me
in his hands smiling.

Unfortunately now
addiction was his real best friend.
And me, Matthew, I'm on my
hands and knees
crying.

the well-worn vest
M.S.W. Migneault

Old man...

Your vest is well worn—
It has seen better days,
Like when it hung beside your bike
In the middle of the living room
The leather still strong and street black.

Old man...
Your steed has carried you far
Through wind and rain
And narrow pass roads
Hidden in winter's whiteouts
Or clicking and cranking down
While you both rested
In summer campgrounds
Beside rivers and hills
A day's journey up ahead ...

Old man...
Your memories are packed
In saddle bags and photos
Of bike runs to Vermont,
New Hampshire and Maine,
While the horizon of Connecticut
Held you steady with traces
Of your Yankee family ties
And roads that brought you back
Again and again.

Old man…
Your life has twisted into knots
So much lost, never to be replaced
A mean streak fills in the spaces
Left by roads that just led nowhere
Rusting your chrome and stripping love
From your heart like a thief in the night

Old man…
You have forgotten

Soldier
Gloria Mindock
  (from Blood Soaked Dresses, 2007)

I put flowers on imaginary graves.
Especially since I don't know
where the bodies are.

I resent your brutality.
My lips are destroyed.
Skin hangs from my bones, but
still you try to kiss me.
This torture has its advantages —
It reminds me that death is my only warmth.

My wounds are superficial.
I control my words with quietness
which betrays my blood, which wants to escape
from this body and scream with its own voice.

Tell me what you want.
The hourglass is empty.
Forget it, I'll endure.
I will try to sleep when you leave.
I did not bargain for this.
I am hurt, and I am searching for a halo.
In my thoughts I'm laughing
as the world dissolves.

Friend Me

Imogen Nelson

Tinkle of bells as the doors close
Behind me. Scan the room.
An empty table or a seat
At which I can assume

The position. The waiting game.
I must look so alone.
My heel tap-taps, and yet my hands?
Determinedly prone.

She's coming, I swear, or at least
I think. She's always late.
Around me thumbs tap-tap away;
Is that to be my fate?

So scared of seeming lonely, and
Afraid of my own thoughts,
My hand wanders unknowingly
And then there I am not.

Numbly, scrolling through Facebook I've
Returned to my true friends.
Though I'm no longer present,
I am safe from me again.

Safe from looking solitary,
Though that is what I am.
Opinions have no value, but
Tap-taps on Instagram.

Street People
B.Z. Niditch

Crowds at dusk
with better weather
here at "The Club,
Last Rainbow"
some Friday night
when out of town folks
with lighter arms
on shirtsleeve notice
taste the smoke
among the barbeques
in fires of hot stoves
by skinny rows
of street people
listening to my alto sax
on the loudspeaker
along the waterfront
breaking glasses
of wine with waves
for tourist friends
on a boardwalk of trees
where crows try to rest
on park back benches
and a new born
on his father's shoulder
goes berserk with laughter.

Where I Hoped To Find Lorca's Ghost
normal

Somewhere
Beyond the land of Endless
Sunflowers
Somewhere
Before the City of Granada
The old Basque stands
Before his melon truck
Testing proudly the richness
Of his green & yellow prize. The world

Moves the way it wants, but
The bent one taps his fruit,
Giving in not a thing
To the worldly tide
Of modern madness.

"The Center of Power is in its juices"
He says with a parent's smile
Ear to his melon,
"What eases the heart is the
First taste of anything"
He says coyly, slicing the
Fruit in half.

I take a bite.
It is the sweetest fruit I
Have ever eaten.

I pay for the melon
Wave goodbye to the
Grinning Merchant &
Hurry on to the City of Gypsies

Where I am deeply disappointed.

(untitled)
Lin A. Nulman

T-shirt heat. Black-haired
boy's block-print tattoo fills his
forearm: FORGIVEN.

> Early autumn day.
> Bronze beads pepper a bench from
> a broken earring.

To Sleep
Siobhan O'Connor

In a rain of feathers
In a furrowed field
In a grave of lilies
Fields of new petals and birds

In sleep a surcease
Spring and summer glint
On the boughs overripe
Seasons spun in dreams
Glimpses of glimmering wings
Folding and unfolding

In the dark cave of myself
Speaking to myself
I rise on a breath of light
In fields of gathered words
I rise with echoing throat

In the hours of glass
When all reflections pain me
When I could weep
And not be heard
The wind in the lilies
stir in me my heart —

When I am asleep
In dream-planted hours
the wings echo in my throat
And the feathers sing
In the grave of the hour.

City Scape
By Chad Parenteau

Come so far
catching up.

Nothing saved,
knowing
not every passerby
gang member
prostitute.

When young
friends warned
Hare Krishnas
cut unbelievers
come nightfall
unseen
in while.

Hit me and I'll sue
makes own
middle ground
on Mass Ave.

Traffic checks
if university ways
need wave be straight.

On Newbury,
reggae-singing beggar
coins percussion,
weathers New England.

Make-up
oranges face
before lifting
awning.

Remainder
left to remind:
Always do more
than survive.

lawmaker destroys shopping carts
Marge Piercy

The homeless make him angry.
They're in the way. He doesn't
find them scenic. How dare they
survive on the street, in parks,
in alleys, doorways and beaches.

Making life even more difficult
for those at the end of choices
is his answer to their problems.
Euthanasia would likely please
him. Has he never lost a job?

Run out of money? Been robbed
or beaten? Never been hungrier
than a good steak fixed? He can't
understand how people scrape,
pick trash to survive, pushing

all that remains of their past
in a shopping cart. Their lives
aren't hard enough, he thinks,
planning how to vanish them
taking the little they have left.

Keep Your Coins, I Want Change
Eddie "Sorez" Pliska

For the homeless one
Nothing shall change
At the stroke of midnight
People will still point
Laugh and stare
As he begs for change
Rummaging through garbage cans
His face sullen
Clothes torn and tattered
In the morning
He will awaken
In a cardboard box
His only shelter
Nothing shall change
For him this New Year
Others will go on their way
Living their lives
Without caring
Pompous individuals, fools,
Blind leading the blind
Deaf and dumb
For they do not realize
The homeless one
They have mocked
Throughout centuries
Is the chosen one
The millennium man
Sent by God above
To see if this wretched world
Is truly worth saving

The Secret of Happiness
Bill Roberts

Sorry now that I ran into you,
finding you so down,
you finding me so up
that you said so —

Gee, you look like
the happiest guy
in America.
How do you do it?

Truth is, I didn't know
I looked happy,
that happy, anyway.
Didn't know I was happy.

Now that you've mentioned it,
I'm suddenly depressed,
not having thought of
my state of being before seeing you.

It reminds me of an old axiom
I can't quite quote, but it goes
sort of like this — you're happiest
when you don't think about it.

SUICIDE IS PREVENTABLE
Mary Esther Rohman

Suicide is preventable.
We didn't really want to die
But how else can you stop the pain?

All I had was pain
Pain like blackness.
Hurt and anger, folded into depression.
No way to get out
But the way I came in.

I was born into the darkness
Thinking someone else's thoughts.
They were so familiar
I thought they were mine.

They occupied my mind
Like a foreign army
Unbidden and unwanted.
Until good people
Who inhabited this otherwise
Hostile territory
Taught me how to think
My own thoughts.
That made me strong
Strong enough to climb stairs
To places where my thoughts were safe.

I made friends with my anger
It was only thoughts
Put there by people with bad intent.
None of them mine.
I was only a child
An innocent in the darkness
Looking for the underground railroad
To the place where
I would learn I wasn't my fault.

And the anger collapsed in on itself
Like over risen dough.
I punched it down
Shaped it to my liking
And baked it so it would
Never grow again.
We ate the darkness for dinner.
It tasted home-made.

My mother taught me how to cook.
But she didn't make it out alive.
But it's okay.
I know the recipe now.

The army left my mind
To the good people.
There is no more rage and darkness.
Just shades of grey
Like my hair
It's turning silver
Shining like the sun.

Argument
Julie Scanga

Every single stripe flowing with loops of color
Music notes swinging to the strength of our necks
Two turkeys on Mass Ave. depending on the moment
Past those baby blues I search a train track
I can't imagine the shoes you see

A baby, a baby fastened to the back of a wigwam
The coils of my blue black hair climbing your face
To re-root in your head

Every pulse boom-boom, a drum or a smack
Never climbing to discover an independent nature
The blood of your lips informing me of our state
We go here, we go there, tearing out our hair
Beautiful as it had to be, the madness ensued
The breath of our silver strike

All along the sidewalk I see demons and wonder
Why you walk faster, do you see like me?

Simpatico Ideal
Julie Kate Scanga

Against you, before me, behind you
To dance!
Motion of the ocean, glitter and expanse
Trade you, to fade you, to rush and embrace
The snow and the mountain caps,
Mars-Jupiter space!
Beginning to end, the colors to trance
To rise and to fall, the current of love
Turning, spinning, below and above
A relation of beauty, moving unbridled
The gesture unfettered, an elegant spiral

i've yet miles to ride
L.P. Scerri

Saddle bags are packed
That old bed roll is tied
First light of day
I'll be on my way
I've yet miles to ride

Time to say goodbye babe
Lord knows we both tried
No guilt, no blame
Now the wind calls my name
I've yet miles to ride

A gypsy seed has taken root
Where once my heart reside
Its reason and rhyme
All in due time
I've yet miles to ride

Mirrors and wrinkles reflect a life
Mile markers and years ever astride
That being said
There's road left ahead
I've yet miles to ride

As my last kickstand is set
Standing before those who preside
I'll be smiling, 'cause ya know
Wherever they tell me to go
I've yet miles to ride

Memories in the Snow
Lainie Senechal

The sun reappears;
storm after storm has
moved out, over the sea.
Snow on branches
shimmers in the wind;
drops of silver
like small meteors
fall to earth.
A white heart with shiny bells
hangs on the tree, a souvenir
from our trip to Montreal,
more a wedding favor
than a holiday ornament;
a reminder of your reply.
"No matter what happens we will
always remember these days."
What was not revealed:
memories would be
all that remained
like dry and brittle
leaves of oak
which fly along the snow.
Only empty space
in the places that you filled.
Hands have nothing to grasp
not even the reason why.

You were always a space traveler
heading out to distant places
along paths you alone would choose.
Love was not enough
to hold you here.
I walk the white landscape,
as pure as a funeral shroud,
the sound of a distant train
reminds me that you
have left us and moved on.

A HOBO'S LAMENT
Eddie Sorez

Having paved my way
Now trying
To find my place
Upon this dirt
Wondering wandering
Alone again finding
Hobo's comfort out of
Tin cans besides
Drums fire fueled
By yesterdays news
Finding myself besides
Those such as me alone
Just trying to stay warm

reflections from the road
Jake St. John

I cannot sleep tonight
stars scream in my eyes
the train horn tosses
and turns in my bed
invisible children
stomachs as empty
as their dreams
whimpering
in the rush of night
homeless clutching
cardboard resumes
and coffee cups
void of hope
fragile voices
asking my nightmares
for change

Winters End
Fred Steele

I feel the bitter edge of winter
As the season nears its end
I see round every corner
Round every rocky bend
I am looking for a melody
To make the season rhyme
As I watch the season melting
One snowflake at a time

The Battle of The Bards
Paul Steven Stone

It was billed as a ten round fight
Between two aging poets
Who could punch out the lights,
In one corner Doug Holder
Whose poems and bon mots
Grew hot as the night grew older,
In the other, with sheets of verse
Marc D. Goldfinger was ready
To scratch and claw for the purse,
It was billed as a ten round night
But in the end, only one poet
Would be standing aright.

It began as most slugfests do
With sharp tongues keeping time
In a strange pas de deux,
The man suspendered in red
Drew first blood with words
Some other poet had bred,
Then Holder raised a clenched fist
To read from pages of white
The first poem on his list,
And thus a mighty battle ensued
Between two gray-beard poets
In a gallery of blue.

Oh, to watch these wizened old men
Parry and feint and dance
As if they were young again,
Goldfinger under his hat
Takes a swing at Holder
with an ode to Kerouac,
Holder, still standing tall
Recalls his youth and
The Long Island sprawl,
There are poems of all stripes,
Tales of junkies, beggars and egos
Do battle through the night.

And I, perched on my hard seat
Finally realize just who
These warriors of words hoped to beat,
It was not each other they faced

But Father Time whose traces
No poem could erase,
And when the battle was done
So that all weary fans
Could trembling head home
We would recall this poets' fight
And with wistful gratitude
What they both had won tonight.

Bookmaking
David R. Surette

One of the Felician Sisters
at Our Lady of Czestochowa
my mother's second grade teacher, was telling
the school kids about the value of books.
They were to be loved, covered, and cared for.
My mother saw her opportunity
and bragged, "My father is a bookmaker!"

He was, and he figured the odds
on happiness with a woman
who struggled with happy
and sad, and he left her, and
my mother and her brother
(who wasn't his)
to be split up,
passed through
foster homes and relatives' arms.

He died at 95, good news for my genes.
He hadn't seen my mother since she
was 24 and appeared at his bar to show
him how well she turned out,
pictures of my brother and me as proof.
He had already cashed out.

We didn't go to the wake or funeral,
and we go to everyone's.
We figured the over and under of whether
it would make my mother happy or sad
and skipped it.

Copper Beech
Maria Termini

I sit on the porch steps I'm repairing,
relaxed, enjoying the shade
of a huge copper beech.

This tree fills the front yard
with metallic radiance,
exploding higher than the house.

Today in the noonday sun,
the full-leafed tree shimmers and glows,
with deep red flashes and hints of green.
Branches swirl off a thick twisted trunk
becoming a tabernacle of colored glory,
opening to cardinals and sparrows alike,
landing in its radiant splendor.

The home owner has recently become blind,
but I know she will want to know about this tree
and I will tell her.

POW
Meg Turner

After Patton came (and yes how often you told us
You were close enough to touch him)
You carried it
On a long journey of liberation across Europe
A wing over the ocean and a final ferry
From New Jersey to Staten Island

Finally home
To your waiting wife, infant daughter and
Warm bright kitchen
The large grey tin spoon
You ate with (or often not) each day in prison camp

With it you served up
Not just our daily vegetables
But bowls of hope
Platters of gratitude
And many, many spoonfuls of play

We were fed by your memory
The suffering and the joy
— Oh your delight in fun —
Cherishing every simple day

So when we gathered for your last crossing
We honored you through what you spoke to us:
"Remember each day is a good day
When the doorknob is on your side of the door."

Colleen *(May 1989 — September 2013)*
Lee Varon

I know your name now
I know you have no place
to sleep tonight.
I know you're so anxious
you can't come and sit
with the other guests
so I bring you a meal-to-go.
Don't give her money
someone says
I give you chicken
rice, an orange.

Your beauty is dissolving
into night,
smack, skag, snow, H
taking you.

Heroin is white
         but your lips are blue
and blue is seeping into the room
where you passed out last week,
the room
where your head hit the floor,
blue dust is wafting from the ceiling,
oozing from the floorboards,

Blue like your scarred veins
         begging for oblivion.

At the end of your life
   a blue
         question mark.

VODKA
Andrew Warburton

The bottle kicked by her black-stockinged foot
spilled no vodka. We'd drunk it all.
You saw our backs rotating on the floor.

My soft tongue was not shaped for the rough
dog-flesh between her legs.
The scorching of her zip.

I told you her lemon zest
was on my lips.
There was horror in your eyes.
The ice cut asymmetrically
on Moscow river
would surely cool this shame.

Or vodka. The unique sound
of splitting cubes.

On Cambridge Common
Molly Lynn Watt

Students hustle by but do not see him
alone on the park bench taking a smoke
Years ago he was a student on his way to somewhere
Now he spends his days on the Common
his silver hair pulled out of the way in a pony-tail
always the same frayed jeans and shirt
gray sneakers tied with string
A canvas case patched with duct tape sits beside him
he lifts out a battered 12-string guitar
its bridge stressed out from years of percussive picking —
glances at the faint autographs on its leather back strap
Josh White, Guy Carawan, Pete Seeger, Tony Saletan —
places his still-burning cigarette between two strings
adjusts the tuning pegs, strums to find a key
hums as his feet tap out the beat and sings
This world is not my home, I'm just a-passing through…

His lips curl into a smile around the sounds
as he sings to a galaxy of ghosts
He is not worrying about sifting through trash cans
for discarded chips, half-eaten sandwiches
nor finding a place to sleep on a bench, behind a bush
or with some young woman happening his way
willing to share her dorm bed for a night of song
Tomorrow he will drift off to another bench
shrouded in the proud tradition of protest
to rage against hard times, lost causes, corrupt bosses
mine disasters, union strikes, unjust wars, parted lovers
not thinking of the wife and babies he left behind
He pauses for a nip from his monogrammed flask
The angels beckon me from Heaven's open door
And I can't feel at home in this world anymore…

Passing By
Richard Wilhelm
  (from his book Awakenings)

I walk past
a mother pushing
her child
in a stroller
on a bright
June morning.
They are sweetly
singing together
"We All Live
In a Yellow Submarine."
Farther up the path,
the sparrows have gathered
in a single bush
and are behaving
riotously.

About Words
MarySusan Williams-Migneault

My nana loved books
it seemed to me
she grew them
in her room
I would listen
to words
I didn't know
but somehow Nana
wrapped her love
around each word
and stored them
in my soul....

I don't remember
what was read
or why or when
she chose
the books she did
their secret meaning
like bulbs planted
their roots deeply hid
embedded in my mind
under layers of ignorance
shoots of Nana's wisdom
fertilized by experience
pushing ever upwards
through the soul
to be harvested
by my pen...

Homeless

A. D. Winans

He stands in the rain searching
Garbage bins for pieces of treasure
An edible half finished sandwich
A piece of day old bread
Aluminum recyclable cans
Which he packs
In his shopping-cart
His home on wheels limping
Limping off into the night
Talking to the cracks in the street.

Illegal
A.D. Winans

she sits alone in her small hotel room
six months pregnant
forced to give head for soup and bread
 no heat, one wash clothe, one towel
one urine-stained washbasin
an immigrant without a visa
an illegal caught in a legal trap

she gets up
heads for the door
hears the night manager whisper whore
suspended in silence floating
face down in the bowels of the
American dream.